365
QUOTES
by

MAHATMA
GANDHI

Om Books International

This edition first published in 2016 by

Om Books International

Corporate & Editorial Office
A-12, Sector 64, Noida 201 301
Uttar Pradesh, India
Phone: +91 120 477 4100
Email: editorial@ombooks.com
Website: www.ombooksinternational.com

Sales Office
107, Ansari Road, Darya Ganj,
New Delhi 110 002, India
Phone: +91 11 4000 9000
Fax: +91 11 2327 8091
Email: sales@ombooks.com
Website: www.ombooks.com

This edition copyright © Om Books International 2016

Compiled by Aparna Kumar

Designed by Arijit Ganguly

ISBN: 978-93-85609-93-0

Printed in India

10 9 8 7 6 5 4 3 2 1

INTRODUCTION

In 1893, Mohandas Karamchand Gandhi, serving as legal counsel in South Africa, was thrown off a train on the insistence of a white man, despite having a first-class ticket. Gandhi fought back — one of his earliest acts of civil disobedience against racial discrimination. Years after this life-altering experience, Gandhi returned to a colonised India in 1914. He spearheaded the freedom movement through non-cooperation, non-violence (Ahimsa), Satyagraha (insistence on truth) and self-rule (Swaraj); and on 15th August, 1947, India gained independence from British rule. Popularly known as Bapu and The Father of the Nation, this simple, dhoti-clad and charkha-spinning leader of the masses fell to an assassin's bullets on 30th January, 1948.

This compendium includes Mahatma Gandhi's inspirational quotes on love, truth and justice.

There are
innumerable
definitions of God,
because His
manifestations are
innumerable.

Man, as soon as
he gets back his
consciousness of right,
is thankful to the
Divine mercy
for an escape.

A clean confession,
combined with a
promise never to
commit the sin again,
when offered before
one who has
the right to receive it,
is the purest type
of repentance.

A man of truth
must also
be a man
of care.

A vow is a vow.
It cannot be broken.

If you don't find God in the next person you meet, it's a waste of time looking further.

No one can ride the back of a man unless it is bent.

Strength in numbers is the delight of the timid. The valiant in spirit glory in fighting alone.

There are some actions
from which an escape
is a godsend both for
the man who escapes
and for those
about him.

Even though a man often succumbs to temptation, however much he may resist it, Providence often intercedes and saves him in spite of himself.

Plain living

harmonised my inward

and outward life.

No matter

how explicit the

pledge, people will

turn and twist the

text to suit their

own purposes.

Man eats not
for enjoyment
but to live.

True
knowledge
is impossible
without a Guru.

Supplication, worship, prayer are no superstition; they are acts more real than the acts of eating, drinking, sitting or walking.

Morality is the basis of

things, and that truth is the

substance of all morality.

One golden rule

is to accept the

interpretation

honestly put on the

pledge by the party

administering it.

He who seeks

truth alone easily

follows the golden

rule. He need not seek

learned advice for

interpretation.

A convert's
enthusiasm for his
new religion is greater
than that of a person
who is born in it.

Silence is part of the spiritual discipline of a votary of truth.

Accept the
interpretation of
the weaker party,
where there are
two interpretations
possible.

Proneness to exaggerate,

to suppress or modify

the truth, wittingly or

unwittingly, is a natural

weakness of man

and silence is

necessary in order

to surmount it.

A man of few words

will rarely be thoughtless

in his speech;

he will measure

every word.

Of the thing that sustains

him through trials, man

has no inkling, much less

knowledge, at the time.

If an unbeliever, he will

attribute his safety to

chance. If a believer,

he will say

God saved him.

All this talking can
hardly be said
to be of any
benefit to the
world. It is
so much waste of time.

Worship or prayer is no
flight of eloquence; it is no
lip-homage. It springs from
the heart.

Service which is
rendered without joy
helps neither the servant
nor the served. When
it is done for show or for
fear of public opinion,
it stunts the man and
crushes his spirit.

Prayer is an unfailing means
of cleaning the heart of
passions. But it must be
combined with the utmost
humility.

We achieve
purity of the
heart when it is
'emptied of all
but love'.

Prayer needs no speech. It is itself independent of any sensuous effort.

I do not seek

redemption from

the consequences

of my sin. I seek to

be redeemed from sin

itself, or rather from

the very thought

of sin.

An imperfect teacher
may be tolerable
in mundane
matters,
but not in
spiritual matters.

It is good to see

ourselves as others

see us.

Only a perfect gnani deserves

to be enthroned as Guru.

There must, therefore,

be ceaseless

striving after

perfection.

It is easy to stand in

a crowd but it takes

courage to stand alone.

Infinite striving after
perfection is one's
right. It is its own
reward. The rest is in
the hands of God.

Facts mean

truth, and once we

adhere to truth,

the law comes

to our aid

naturally.

The heart's earnest
and pure desire is
always fulfilled.

I had made the

religion of service my

own, as I felt that God

could be realised only

through service.

I found myself

in search of God

and striving for

self-realisation.

Everyone holds a

piece of truth.

Silence becomes cowardice when the occasion demands speaking out the whole truth and acting accordingly.

All other pleasures and possessions pale into nothingness before service which is rendered in a spirit of joy.

What barrier is there that love cannot break?

A patriot cannot

afford to ignore any

branch of service to

the motherland.

The ultimate result

of my experiments is

in the womb of the

future.

Judging a man

from his outward

act is no more than

a doubtful inference,

inasmuch as it is

not based on

sufficient data.

Each night when I go
to sleep, I die. And
the next morning,
when I wake up, I am
reborn.

My experience has shown me that we win justice quickest by rendering justice to the other party.

You cannot shake hands

with a clenched fist.

Champions are made from something that they have deep inside of them — a desire, a dream, a vision.

Non-possession and equability presuppose a change of heart, a change of attitude.

'I do not want to bind myself with vows,' is the mentality of weakness and betrays a subtle desire for the thing to be avoided.

Where the desire

is gone, a vow of

renunciation

is the

natural and

inevitable fruit.

The mind is at the root of all sensuality.

The deeper the search

in the mine of truth, the

richer the discovery of the

gems buried there, in the

shape of openings for an

ever greater variety

of service.

The golden rule of conduct is mutual toleration.

The more helpless a creature, the more entitled it is to protection by man from the cruelty of man. But he who has not qualified himself for such service is unable to afford to it any protection.

Truth is
like a vast tree,
which yields more and
more fruit, the more
you nurture it.

How heavy is the toll

of sins and wrongs

that wealth, power

and prestige exact

from man!

I am definitely

of the opinion that a

public worker should

accept no costly gifts.

To my mind, the life
of a lamb is no less
precious than that of
a human being.

God could be

realised only

through service.

Liberty and democracy become unholy when their hands are dyed red with innocent blood.

No matter what
amount of work
one has, one should
always find some time
to exercise, just as one
does for one's meals.

There is a Supreme Being

hidden therein as a Certainty,

and one would be blessed if

one could catch a

glimpse of that

Certainty and

hitch one's

wagon to it.

He who runs to the doctor, vaidya or hakim for every little ailment, and swallows all kinds of vegetable and mineral drugs, not only curtails his life, but by becoming the slave of his body instead of remaining its master, loses self-control, and ceases to be a man.

It is idle to expect

one's children and

wards necessarily

to follow the same

course of evolution

as oneself.

I think it is
wrong to expect
certainties in this
world, where all else
but God that is Truth,
is an uncertainty.

All that appears and happens

about and around us is

uncertain and

transient.

In refusing

to take a vow, man is

drawn into temptation.

Physical relationship divorced

from spiritual is body

without soul.

Writing is itself

one of the experiments

with truth.

It has always

been a mystery

to me how men can feel

themselves honoured by

the humiliation of their

fellow beings.

A thousand candles can be lighted from the flame of one candle, and the life of the candle will not be shortened.

Fearlessness is the first
requisite of spirituality.

Ahimsa is the

basis of the

search for Truth.

The search is

vain unless

it is founded

on Ahimsa as

the basis.

The institution that
fails to win public
support has
no right
to exist
as such.

The existence of God within makes even control of the mind possible. Let no one think that it is impossible because it is difficult. It is the highest goal, and it is no wonder that the highest effort should be necessary to attain it.

For the seeker

who would live in fear

of God and who would see

Him face to face, restraint

in diet both as to quantity

and quality is as essential

as restraint in thought

and speech.

Ahimsa is a comprehensive principle.

If one's heart is pure,
calamity brings in its train
men and measures to fight it.

Man and his deed are
two distinct things.
Whereas a good
deed should call forth
approbation and wicked
deed disapprobation, the
doer of the deed, whether
good or wicked always
deserves respect or pity
as the case may be.

To slight a single human being is to slight the divine powers, and thus to harm not only that being but with him, the whole world.

I have not seen Him, neither have I known Him. I have made the world's faith in God my own, and as my faith is ineffaceable, I regard that faith as amounting to experience.

When two nations are
fighting, the duty of a votary
of Ahimsa is to
stop the war.

God always
protects the honest
experimenter.

Just as an

unchained torrent

of water submerges

the whole countryside

and devastates crops,

an uncontrolled pen

serves but to destroy.

A poet is one who

can call forth the good latent

in the human breast.

The useful and
the useless must,
like good and evil
generally, go on together,
and man must make
his choice.

Any number of

experiments is too

small and no sacrifice

is too great for

attaining symphony

with nature.

A votary of truth

must exercise the

greatest caution. To

allow a man to believe

a thing which one has

not fully verified is to

compromise truth.

Passion in man is generally co-existent with a hankering after the pleasures of the palate.

We are not ashamed
to sacrifice a multitude
of other lives in decorating
the perishable body and
trying to prolong it existence
for a few fleeting moments,
with the result that we kill
ourselves, both body and soul.

Poets do not influence

all alike, for everyone

is not evolved in an

equal measure.

If anyone doubts the infinite

mercy of God, let him have a

look at sacred places.

In trying to cure one
old disease, we give rise
to a hundred new ones;
in trying to enjoy the
pleasures of the senses,
we lose in the end
even our capacity
for enjoyment.

A votary of Ahimsa
remains true to his
faith if the spring of all
his actions is compassion, if
he shuns to the best of his
ability the destruction of
the tiniest creature, tries to
save it, and thus incessantly
strives to be free from the
deadly coil of Himsa.

If physical fasting
is not accompanied
by mental fasting, it
is bound to end in
hypocrisy and
disaster.

Fasting can help

to curb animal passion,

only if it is undertaken

with a view to self-restraint.

For those whose
minds are working
towards self-restraint,
dietetic restrictions
and fasting are very
helpful.

Because underlying
Ahimsa is the unity
of all life, the error of
one cannot but affect
all, and hence man
cannot be wholly free
from Himsa .

The true

connotation of humility

is self-effacement.

I make no
distinction,
from the point
of view of
Ahimsa, between
combatants and
non-combatants.

He who has no power of resisting war, he who is not qualified to resist war, may take part in war, and yet whole-heartedly try to free himself, his nation and the world from war.

Service without

humility is selfishness

and egotism.

A devotee of Truth
may not do anything
in deference to
convention. He must
always hold himself
open to correction, and
whenever he discovers
himself to be wrong,
he must confess it at all
costs and atone for it.

God can never be

realised by one who is

not pure of heart.

Doubt is invariably

the result of want or

weakness of faith.

Self-effacement is moksha, and whilst it cannot, by itself, be an observance, there may be other observances necessary for its attainment.

If the acts of an
aspirant after moksha
or a servant have no
humility or selflessness
about them, there is no
longing for moksha
or service.

Identification with
everything that lives is
impossible without
self-purification, without
self-purification the
observance of the law of
Ahimsa must remain an
empty dream.

The ideal of truth
requires that vows
taken should be
fulfilled in spirit as
well as in letter.

To attain to perfect purity one has to become absolutely passion-free in thought, speech and action; to rise above the opposing currents of love and hatred, attachment and repulsion.

Every moment of my life
I realise that God is putting
me on my trial.

The path of
self-purification is
hard and steep.

A man who aspires

after truth cannot afford to

keep out of any field of life.

Live simply so that others may simply live.

To see the universal
and all-pervading
Spirit of Truth face-
to-face one must be able
to love the meanest of
creation as oneself.

Self-purification

must mean purification

in all the walks of life.

Purification of
oneself necessarily
leads to the purification
of one's surroundings.

Join with me in prayer

to the God of Truth

that He may grant me

the boon of Ahimsa

in mind, word

and deed.

There is no other God

than Truth.

To develop the spirit

is to build character

and to enable one

to work towards

knowledge of God

and self-realisation.

Let every young

man and woman

be warned by my

example, and understand

that good handwriting

is a necessary part of

education.

Action expresses
priorities.

Jealousy
does not wait for
reasons.

Children should first
be taught the art
of drawing before
learning how to write.

If I have the belief that
I can do it, I shall surely
acquire the capacity to
do it even if I may
not have it at the
beginning.

Non-violence is a

weapon of the strong.

It is difficult, but not impossible, to conduct strictly honest business.

To lose patience is to lose the battle.

The real difficulty

is that people have

no idea what true

education really is.

It is unwise to be too
sure of one's own
wisdom. It is healthy
to be reminded that
the strongest might
weaken and the
wisest might err.

Victory attained

by violence

is tantamount

to a defeat, for

it is momentary.

First they ignore you,

then they laugh at you,

then they fight you,

then you win.

The future

depends on

what you do today.

An ounce of practice

is worth a

thousand words.

You may never know

what results come

of your action, but

if you do nothing

there will be

no result.

Truthfulness in the practice
of the profession cannot
cure it of the fundamental
defect that vitiates it.

Be the change

you want to see

in the world.

Honest differences are
often a healthy sign
of progress.

Hate the sin,
love the sinner.

The best way to find

yourself is to lose yourself

in the service of others.

Service which is rendered

without joy helps

neither the servant

nor the served.

Whatever you do will be

insignificant, but it

is very important

that you do it.

Live as if you were

to die tomorrow.

Learn as if you

were to live forever.

A 'No' uttered from

the deepest conviction

is better than a 'Yes'

merely uttered

to please, or

worse, to

avoid trouble.

Freedom is not

worth having if it

does not include the

freedom to make

mistakes.

You can chain me,

you can torture me,

you can even destroy

this body, but

you will never

imprison

my mind.

Civilisation is the encouragement of differences.

God has given me

no control over the

following moment.

I am concerned

about taking care

of the present.

Happiness is when what you think, what you say, and what you do are in harmony.

The good man is the friend of all living things.

Intolerance is itself a
form of violence and
an obstacle to the
growth of a true
democratic spirit.

If you want

real peace in the

world, start with

children.

No culture can live,

if it attempts

to be exclusive.

The hardest heart

and the grossest

ignorance must

disappear before

the rising sun

of suffering

without anger

and without malice.

That service is the noblest
which is rendered for
its own sake.

Whenever you are confronted
with an opponent, conquer
him with love.

The weak can never forgive. Forgiveness is the attribute of the strong.

To believe in something, and not to live it, is dishonest.

Have faith in
humanity. Humanity
is like an ocean; if
a few drops of the
ocean are dirty, the
whole ocean doesn't
become dirty.

A perfect vision of Truth
can only follow a complete
realisation of Ahimsa.

Even if you are
a minority of one,
the truth is the truth.

A man is but the product of his thoughts. What he thinks, he becomes.

I believe that there

is no prayer without

fasting and there

is no real

fast without

prayer.

Seek not greater wealth
but simpler pleasure;
not higher fortune but
deeper felicity.

An eye for an eye will
only make the whole
world blind.

Your beliefs become your thoughts, Your thoughts become your words, Your words become your actions, Your actions become your habits, Your habits become your values, Your values become your destiny.

Prayer is the key of the morning and the bolt of the evening.

I have no disciples,
being myself an aspirant
after discipleship and
in search of a guru.

Nothing is so aggravating
as calmness.

Non-violence is the

greatest force at the

disposal of mankind.

Always aim at complete
harmony of thought and
word and deed. Always
aim at purifying your
thoughts and
everything will
be well.

To give pleasure to
a single heart by a
single act is better
than a thousand heads
bowing in prayer.

It is easier to build a
boy than mend a man.

Speak only if it improves
upon silence.

I wish to change their

minds, not kill them

for weaknesses

we all possess.

I call him religious who

understands the suffering

of others.

One can measure the greatness and the moral progress of a nation by looking at how it treats its animals.

My life is my message.

An error does
not become truth by
reason of multiplied
propagation, nor does
truth become error
because nobody
sees it.

Earth provides enough

to satisfy every man's

needs, but not even

one man's greed.

Fear has its use but
cowardice has none.

Satisfaction lies in the effort,
not in the attainment. Full
effort is full victory.

There is no 'way to peace';

there is only 'peace'.

Nobody can hurt me

without my permission.

A principle is

the expression of

perfection, and as

imperfect beings like

us cannot practise

perfection, we devise

every moment, limits

of its compromise

in practice.

Distinguish between real

needs and artificial wants

and control the latter.

Compassion is a

muscle that gets

stronger with use.

When I despair, I remember that all through history, the way of Truth and love have always won.

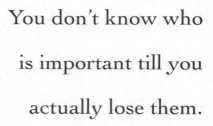

You don't know who

is important till you

actually lose them.

Strength does not come from

physical capacity. It comes

from an indomitable will.

A small body

of determined

spirits fired by

an unquenchable

faith in their

mission can alter

the course

of history.

As long as you derive

inner help and comfort

from anything, keep it.

All humanity is
one undivided and
indivisible family,
and each one of us
is responsible for
the misdeeds of all
the others.

The difference
between what we do
and what we are
capable of doing
would suffice to solve
most of the
world's problem.

I am prepared to die, but there is no cause for which I am prepared to kill.

Before the throne
of the Almighty,
man will be judged
not by his acts but
by his intentions. For
God alone reads
our hearts.

When you want to
find Truth as God,
the only inevitable
means is love,
that is non-violence.

We have to

hand over the earth,

the air, the land and

the water to the

children at least as

it was handed

over to us.

You may never know
what results come of
your actions, but if you
do nothing, there will
be no results.

Faith is put to the test

when the situation is

most difficult.

Love is the strongest force the world possesses, yet it is the humblest imaginable.

Nothing has saddened me so much in life as the hardness of heart of educated people.

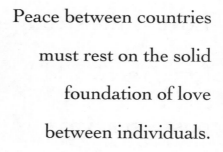

Peace between countries
must rest on the solid
foundation of love
between individuals.

Peace is the most

powerful weapon

of mankind.

Power based on
love is a thousand
times more effective
and permanent
than the one
derived from
fear of
punishment.

True beauty after all consists in purity of heart.

God lives, but not
as we. His creatures
live but to die. But
God is life. Therefore,
goodness is not an
attribute. Goodness
is God.

Anger is the enemy of non-violence and pride is a monster that swallows it up.

In matters of conscience, the law of the majority has no place.

To answer brutality with brutality is to admit one's moral and intellectual bankruptcy.

Non-violence requires a double faith—faith in God and also faith in man.

One needs to be slow to form
convictions, but once formed
they must be defended against
the heaviest odds.

Where there
is love, there
is life.

What is truth? A difficult question; but I have solved it for myself by saying that it is what the 'Voice within' tells you.

I believe in the fundamental
truth of all great religions of
the world.

There is

more to life

than increasing

its speed.

I object to violence
because when it
appears to do good,
the good is only
temporary; the evil it
does is permanent.

The real love is to love them that hate you, to love your neighbour even though you distrust him.

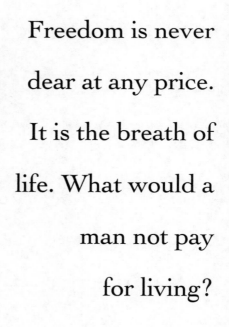

Freedom is never
dear at any price.
It is the breath of
life. What would a
man not pay
for living?

A man is the sum of his actions, of what he has done, of what he can do, nothing else.

Faith becomes lame, when it ventures into matters pertaining to reason!

It is easy enough
to be friendly to
one's friends but to
befriend one who
regards himself as
your enemy is the
quintessence of
true religion.

I feel stronger for confession.

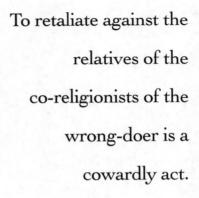

To retaliate against the
relatives of the
co-religionists of the
wrong-doer is a
cowardly act.

Honest disagreement

is often a good sign of

progress.

True education must correspond to the surrounding circumstances or it is not a healthy growth.

Ashram means a community
of men of religion. I feel
that an ashram was
a necessity of
life for me.

It is health that is real
wealth and not pieces
of gold and silver.

Morality which depends

upon the helplessness of

a man or woman has not

much to recommend it.

Morality is rooted

in the purity of

our hearts.

Religion is a matter

of the heart.

A coward is incapable of

exhibiting love; it is the

prerogative of the brave.

There is a higher court

than courts of justice

and that is the court

of conscience.

It supercedes

all other courts.

A leader is useless when he
acts against the promptings
of his own conscience.

You must never despair of human nature.

A nation's culture resides in the hearts and in the soul of its people.

When I admire
the wonders of a
sunset or the beauty
of the moon, my
soul expands in the
worship of
the Creator.

It may be possible to gild pure gold, but who can make his mother more beautiful.

Those who know how to think, need no teachers.

Is it not
enough to know the evil
to shun it? If not, we
should be sincere enough
to admit that we love evil
too well to give it up.

My religion is based on
truth and non-violence.
Truth is my God.
Non-violence is
the means of
realising
Him.

Man's happiness really lies
in contentment.

In a gentle way, you
can shake the world.

There is no God higher

than Truth.

Each one has to find his peace from within. And peace to be real must be unaffected by outside circumstances.

I suppose leadership at one time meant muscles, but today it means getting along with people.

There is orderliness in the universe, there is an unalterable law governing everything and every being that exists or lives. It is no blind law; for no blind law can govern the conduct of living beings.

Man is supposed to be the
maker of his destiny.
It is only partly true.
He can make his
destiny, only in so
far as he is allowed
by the Great Power.

Measures must always
in a progressive society
be held superior to men,
who are after all imperfect
instruments, working for
their fulfillment.

A policy is a temporary creed
liable to be changed, but
while it holds good it
has got to be pursued
with apostolic zeal.

When restraint and courtesy
are added to strength, the
latter becomes irresistible.

Man falls from the pursuit
of the ideal of plain living
and high thinking the
moment he wants to
multiply his daily
wants.

I have nothing new
to teach the world.
Truth and Non-
violence are as old
as the hills. All I
have done is to try
experiments in both
on as vast a scale as
I could.

The path is the goal.

Man's nature is not

essentially evil.

Brute nature has

been known to yield

to the influence

of love.

Confession of errors is like a
broom which sweeps away
the dirt and leaves the surface
brighter and clearer.

A living faith will last

in the midst of the

blackest storm.

Non-cooperation with
evil is as much a duty
as is cooperation
with good.

Anger and intolerance
are the enemies of
correct understanding.

Action is no less necessary
than thought to the
instinctive tendencies
of the human frame.

If patience is worth

anything, it must endure

to the end of time.

I reject any religious doctrine that does not appeal to reason and is in conflict with morality.

God, as Truth, has been for me a treasure beyond price. May He be so to every one of us.

Selfishness turns people blind, and by a use of the ambiguous middle they deceive themselves and seek to deceive the world and God.

Prayer is a confession

of one's own unworthiness

and weakness.

An unjust law is itself a species of violence. Arrest for its breach is more so.

Let us all be brave enough to die the death of a martyr, but let no one lust for martyrdom.

Increase of material comforts, it may be generally laid down, does not in any way whatsoever conduce to moral growth.

I look only to the good
qualities of men. Not
being faultless myself,
I won't presume to probe into
the faults of others.

Literacy is not the end
of education or even the
beiginning.

God sometimes does try

to the uttermost those

whom he wishes to bless.

I claim to be a simple individual liable to err like any other fellow mortal. I own, however, that I have humility enough in me to confess my errors and to retrace my steps.

We may have our private opinions but why should they be a bar to the meeting of hearts?

The moment there

is suspicion about

a person's motives,

everything he does

becomes tainted.

Freedom is not worth having

if it does not connote freedom

to err.

There is only one

God and there

are many paths

to him.

The human voice can
never reach the distance
that is covered by the
still small voice of conscience.

For me, every ruler
is alien that defies
public opinion.

We may never be strong enough to be entirely non-violent in thought, word and deed. But we must keep non-violence as our goal and make strong progress towards it.

My fight against
untouchability is a fight
against the impure in
humanity.

Interdependence is
and ought to be as
much the ideal of man
as self-sufficiency.

I have also seen children successfully surmounting the effects of an evil inheritance. That is due to purity being an inherent attribute of the soul.

Non-violence is the first

article of my faith.

It is also the last

article of my creed.

God is, even though

the whole world

denies him. Truth

stands, even if there be

no public support. It is

self-sustained.

It is any day better

to stand erect with a

broken and bandaged

head then to crawl on

one's belly, in order

to be able to save

one's head.

Non-violence and Truth are inseparable and presuppose one another.

All the religions of
the world, while they
may differ in other
respects, unitedly
proclaim that nothing
lives in this world
but Truth.

To say that

a single human being,

because of his birth,

becomes an untouchable,

unapproachable, or invisible,

is to deny God.

God never made man
that he may consider
another man as an
untouchable.

Justice that love gives

is surrender;

justice that

law gives is a

punishment.

Anger, lust and such other

evil passions raging

in the heart are

the real untouchables.

Common sense is
the realised sense
of proportion.

A religion that takes no
account of practical affairs
and does not help to solve
them is no religion.

Purity of
personal life
is the one
indispensable
condition for
building up a
sound education.

But for my faith in God,

I should have been a

raving maniac.

Unwearied ceaseless
effort is the price
that must be paid for
turning faith into a
rich infallible
experience.

There are people in the
world so hungry, that
God cannot appear to
them except in the form
of bread.

Capital as such is not evil; it is its wrong use that is evil. Capital in some form or other will always be needed.

Gentleness, self-sacrifice

and generosity are the

exclusive possession

of no one race or religion.

What is really needed to

make democracy function

is not knowledge of facts,

but right education.

The spirit of democracy is not a mechanical thing to be adjusted by abolition of forms. It requires change of heart.

My religion teaches me that
whenever there is distress
which one cannot remove,
one must fast and pray.

Those who say religion has nothing to do with politics do not know what religion is.

Nearly everything you do is of no importance, but it is important that you do it.

Prayer is not an old woman's idle amusement. Properly understood and applied, it is the most potent instrument of action.

If a man reaches the heart

of his own religion, he has

reached the heart of the

others, too.

Intolerance betrays want
of faith in one's cause.

Violent means will give

violent freedom.

He is lost who is
possessed by
carnal desire.

Love requires that true
education should be easily
accessible to all.

I am in the world feeling

my way to light 'amid the

encircling gloom.'

Literacy in itself

is no education.

One's own religion

is after all a matter

between oneself and

one's Maker and

no one else's

Providence has
its appointed hour
for everything. We
cannot command
results, we can
only strive.

Constant development is the law of life, and a man who always tries to maintain his dogmas in order to appear consistent, drives himself into a false position.

If you want to be a bear,

be a grizzly.

There are two days in the year that we cannot do anything—yesterday and tomorrow.

If we are to teach real peace in this world, and if we are to carry on a real war against war, we shall have to begin with the children.

The main purpose of life is to live rightly, think rightly, and act rightly. The soul must languish when we give all our thought to the body.

There would be nothing to frighten you if you refused to be afraid.

The seeker after truth should be humbler than the dust. The world crushes the dust under its feet, but the seeker after truth should so humble himself that even the dust could crush him. Only then, and not till then, will he have a glimpse of truth.

I can only teach you

not to bow your heads

before anyone even

at the cost of your life.

My aim is not to be consistent

with my previous statements

on a given question, but to be

consistent with truth as it may

present itself to me at a given

moment. The result has been

that I have grown from

truth to truth.

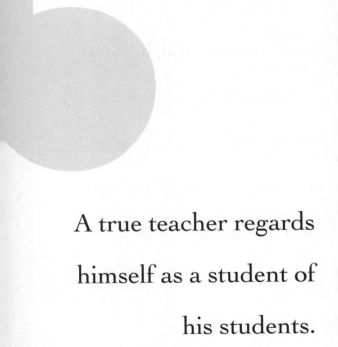

A true teacher regards

himself as a student of

his students.

Men and women
approaching retirement
age should be recycled for
public service work, and
their companies should
foot the bill. We can
no longer afford to
scrap-pile people.

Birth and death are not two different states, but they are different aspects of the same state. There is as little reason to deplore the one as there is to be pleased over the other.

I will not let anyone

walk through my

mind with their

dirty feet.

It is better in prayer

to have a heart without

words than

words without a heart.

It is the duty of every cultured man or woman to read sympathetically the scriptures of the world. If we are to respect others' religions as we would have them respect our own, a friendly study of the world's religions is a sacred duty.

Prayer is not asking.

It is a longing of the soul.

It is daily admission of

one's weakness.

The concupiscence of the mind cannot be rooted out except by intense self-examination, surrender to God and, lastly, grace.

Whenever I talk with someone, I learn from them.

I cannot teach you violence, as I do not believe in it. I can only teach you not to bow your heads before anyone even at the cost of your life.

It is much more difficult to

live for non-violence than

to die for it.

By education I mean
an all-round drawing
out of the best in
the child and man —
body, mind and spirit.

The principle
of majority
does not work
when differences
on fundamentals
are involved.

I do feel that spiritual
progress does demand,
at some stage, that we
should cease to kill our
fellow creatures for
the satisfaction of
our bodily wants.

If we are to make
progress, we must not
repeat history but make
new history.

Many people, especially, ignorant people want to punish you for speaking the truth, for being correct, for being you.

Never apologise
for being correct,
or for being
years ahead of
your time.

As human beings, our

greatness lies not so

much in being able to

remake the world –

that is the myth of the

atomic age – as

in being able to

remake ourselves.

He who learns

nothing from his

disciples, is in my

opinion, worthless.

If you are right, and
you know it, speak
your mind.

Poverty is the worst

form of violence.

I may be a despicable man,

but when Truth speaks

through me, I am invincible.

The day the power of love

overrules the love of power,

the world will know peace.

Man becomes great

exactly in the degree

in which he works

for the welfare of his

fellow-men.

Without action,

you're not going

anywhere.

A student is he who continuously uses his faculty of observation, puts two and two together and carves out for himself a path in life.

Permanent good can never be
the outcome of untruth and
violence.

A customer is the most

important visitor on our

premises.

I am a humble but very earnest seeker after truth.

You yourself as much
as anybody in the entire
universe deserve your
love and affection.

God has no
religion.

The good man is

the friend of all

living things.

Character alone

will have real effect

on the masses.

Self-respect knows

no considerations.

The only tyrant I accept

in this world is the still

voice within.

Faith is not something to

grasp; it is a state to grow into.

Peace is its own

reward.

It is the quality of our work

which will please God and not

the quantity.

Simplicity is the

essence of universality.